D0555491

Cover illustration. Self-propelled artillery pieces were widely
used in Vietnam to provide area coverage from prepared
positions in fire support bases. An M109 155mm self-propelled
howitzer of 11th Armored Cavalry Regiment awaits a fire
mission at Bien Hoa in 1969. (John Graber)

1. ACAVs and Sheridans of Troop K, 3rd Squadron, 11th Armored Cavalry Regiment, prepare to move out on a 'search and destroy' mission in January 1971. Each vehicle follows exactly in the track of the one in front in order to minimise the danger from mines. (US Army)

Tank War Vietnam

SIMON DUNSTAN

ARMS AND ARMOUR PRESS

London – Melbourne – Harrisburg, Pa. – Cape Town

To Joanna

Introduction

Tanks Illustrated 6: Tank War Vietnam
Published in 1983 by
Arms and Armour Press, Lionel Leventhal Limited,
2-6 Hampstead High Street, London NW3 1QQ;
4-12 Tattersalls Lane, Melbourne, Victoria 3000,
Australia; Sanso Centre, 8 Adderley Street,
PO Box 94, Cape Town 8000, South Africa;
Cameron and Kelker Streets, PO Box 1831,
Harrisburg, Pennsylvania 17105, USA.

© Lionel Leventhal Limited, 1983
All rights reserved. No part of this publication may
be reproduced, stored in a retrieval system or
transmitted in any form by any means electrical,
mechanical or otherwise, without first seeking the
written permission of the copyright owner.

British Library Cataloguing in Publication Data:
Dunstan, Simon
Tank war Vietnam.—(Tanks illustrated; 6)
1. United States. *Army*—Armored troops—History
2. Vietnamese conflict, 1961–1975—Tank warfare
I. Title   II. Series
959.704′342   DS558.2
ISBN 0-85368-603-3

Layout by Anthony A. Evans
Typesetting and make-up by
Wyvern Typesetting Limited, Bristol.
Printed in Great Britain by
William Clowes (Beccles) Limited.

The popular conception of the war in Vietnam is limited to the heavily-laden infantryman struggling through slimy, leech-infested paddy fields or dense, hostile jungle and the ubiquitous use of helicopters. Even within professional armies many doubted the use of other types of weapons and tactical concepts in tropical warfare – none more so than the employment of armoured fighting vehicles. Yet, from the outset of the First Indo-China War, the French had used tanks and armoured cars as well as tracked landing vehicles to advantage but had continually suffered a severe shortage of manpower, equipment and support which ultimately led to defeat at the hands of the increasingly powerful forces of the Viet Minh.

Drawing false conclusions from the French experience, the US Army deployed its initial divisions to Vietnam without their mechanized or tank battalions, but the success of the South Vietnamese Army in employing the M113 APC as a light tank persuaded American units to follow suit. Within a short time the M113, and the associated Armored Cavalry Assault Vehicle (ACAV) in its configuration as a fighting vehicle, proved to be the most effective AFV of the war. In support of infantry operations, the M48A3 Patton also proved highly effective and capable of operating throughout large areas of the country. Backing up these principal AFVs of the war were a whole host of others, including a range of tanks, APCs, armoured cars, self-propelled guns and special-purpose vehicles.

The use of AFVs in Vietnam remains a subject of controversy among professional soldiers, but it is indisputable that it was four North Vietnamese Army (NVA) corps spearheaded by hundreds of Soviet T-55 and Chinese T-59 tanks which extinguished the Republic of Vietnam in the spring of 1975.

The majority of photographs are courtesy of the US Army and US Marine Corps Still Photographic Libraries, but the author wishes to thank several other organizations and individuals for their kind assistance in providing material including Arme Blindée et Cavalerie, *Armor* Magazine, Australian War Memorial, George J. Balin, Colonel Raymond R. Battreall Jr., USA (Ret.), Geoff Cornish, Major John P. Graber, USA, Paul Handel, Colonel Stanley E. Holtom, USA (Ret.), Peter de Jong, Doug Lennox, Trevor 'Bluey' Lowe, Tim Page, Royal Australian Armoured Corps, Lieutenant-Colonel Gary L. Solis, USMC, and Steven J. Zaloga.

Simon Dunstan, 1983

2. The standard medium tank used by the USMC was the M48A3, organised in two tank battalions, 1st and 3rd, attached to 1st and 3rd Marine Divisions respectively. An M48A3 of Bravo Company, 1st Tank Battalion, laden with .50in ammunition boxes and C-ration cartons, forges over a rise during an operation in support of 3/7 Marines. Around the turret are two layers of spare trackblocks which afforded some protection against RPGs. (USMC)

▲3

▲4 ▼5

3. The French Expeditionary Corps arrived in Indo-China with a motley selection of wartime AFVs. The standard tank at the outset of this conflict was the M5A1. The M24 Chaffee was supplied as part of the American aid programme but the M5A1 remained in service throughout the war against the Viet Cong. In this photograph, M5A1 of Groupe Mobile 1 shelters in the roadside undergrowth during Operation 'Amphibio', March 1952. (Arme Blindée et Cavalerie)

4. An M8 Howitzer Motor Carriage of the 1er Régiment de Chasseurs à Cheval crosses a stream during the battle of the Black River in support of the 5ème Battalion Parachutistes Coloniaux, December 1951. (ABC)

5. To increase mobility across the numerous swamps and inundated paddy-fields of Vietnam some units were equipped with M29C Weasel Cargo Carriers, called 'Crabers' by the French, which were configured as fighting vehicles armed with machine-guns or recoilless rifles. Here, a Crabe of 1er Escadron, 1er Groupe d'Escadrons Amphibies of 2ème Groupement Amphibie, negotiates a waterway near Nam Dinh in June 1954. (ABC)

6. An M8 Greyhound armoured car of 1er Chasseurs escorts a Dodge ambulance along Route Coloniale near Xom Pheo in Tonkin during the battle of the Black River, December 1951. (ABC)

7. M24 Chaffees of 2ème Escadron, 1er Régiment de Chasseurs à Cheval, return fire in an ambush during Operation 'Mouette' in October 1952. The M24 proved highly effective in Indo-China; it was fast, hard-hitting and manoeuvrable even in the wet season. (ABC)

▲8

8. A Panhard Type 178B armoured car advances along a typical jungle track in Cochinchina during Operation 'Chaumière' in support of 1er Battalion Parachutiste Vietnamien, 1952. Note the vehicle name VERCORS on the glacis plate, and the registration number which comprises the French tricolour, the letters IC (denoting Indo-China) and vehicle number. (ABC)

9. From 1950 the Crabe units were reinforced with LVT-4 Alligators which provided essential troop-carrying capability for extended operations against the Viet Minh. An LVT-4 Alligator traverses muddy terrain during Operation 'Quadrille', July 1952. (ABC)

10. After the Communist victory in neighbouring China in 1949, the French shipped M4 Shermans and M36 Tank Destroyers to Indo-China as a counter to possible attacks by Chinese tanks in support of the Viet Minh. In this photograph the crew of a re-manufactured M4A1 observe an airstrike against enemy positions during an operation in Tonkin in 1951. (ABC)

9▲   10▼

▲11   ▼12

11. The standard armoured personnel carrier used by the French in Indo-China was the redoubtable US halftrack. These M2 halftracks of 3ème Régiment de Reconnaissance Vietnamien have been fitted with rear doors, similar to those on M3, M5 and M8 halftracks, a common French post-war modification. Note the crew kitbags lashed to the carrier with spent machine-gun belts. (ABC)

12. An M36B2 Tank Destroyer of the Régiment Blindé Colonial d'Extrême-Orient climbs a paddy dike near Nam Dinh in Tonkin, February 1954. These vehicles were used for fire support in the absence of enemy tanks. Note the RBCEO unit flag flying from the aerial. (ABC)

13▲ 14▼

13. The M113 APC was introduced into Vietnam in March 1962 and began operations in June in the Mekong Delta, an area of dense mangrove swamps, watercourses and paddy-fields, where the amphibian characteristics of the M113 conferred greatly enhanced mobility to the Army of the Republic of Vietnam (ARVN). (FMC)

14. An ARVN M113 negotiates a French Eiffel bridge during one of the first mobile operations in the Delta region. At the outset the ARVN followed the US Army doctrine of mechanized infantry whereby troops dismounted to assault an objective, but this often proved unworkable in Vietnam, and ARVN troops invariable fought from their carriers. (FMC)

▲15 ▼16

17▲

15. The waterlogged terrain of the Mekong Delta was a severe testing ground for the APCs, where paddy dikes and irrigation channels impeded mobility, but many ingenious methods were devised to overcome the obstacles. These M113s feature side-mounted .30in machine-guns and gunshields for the .50in Browning to increase firepower and protection. (FMC)

16. An M41A3 of 5th Armored Cavalry Regiment advances along a street in Da Nang supported by infantry during the Buddhist revolt in I Corps Tactical Zone, May 1966. The M41 replaced the ageing M24 Chaffees in ARVN tank squadrons during 1965. (Tim Page)

17. On account of the many obstacles encountered in the Mekong Delta and elsewhere, the need arose for a lightweight, vehicle-launched bridge, mounted on an M113. Such a system was designed and developed at Fort Belvoir, Virginia, in the latter half of 1965. It consisted of a rectangular frame fitted to the front of an M113 with standard M4T6 aluminium balk sections from existing engineer equipment carried on top of the vehicle. The carrier stopped some distance from the obstacle; the components were assembled and attached by hand. It then moved forward to launch the bridge by means of a quick-release mechanism operated from the driver's compartment. Although crude, it was effective, and a bridge could be launched with an entire squadron carried across a 30ft gap in less than half an hour, as against three to five hours by previous means. Production of 24 M113 'balk-bridgelayers' was undertaken by ARVN engineers. These were authorised on a scale of one per regimental headquarters in armoured cavalry regiments but were actually used only in the Delta where the frequency of water obstacles justified the dedication of a fighting vehicle to this purpose. (Raymond Battreall)

▲18

▲19 ▼20

18. Of the many expedients devised to enable M113s to negotiate the many watercourses of Vietnam, the 'capstan and anchor' technique of self-recovery was one of the most successful, albeit time-consuming, methods. The kit consisted of two metal drums, or capstans, which were bolted to the drive sprockets, a ground anchor and two 100ft lengths of nylon rope. By placing the anchor in firm ground and attaching the rope to the capstans, the APC wound itself out of difficulty. (US Army)

19. An M113 APC of 3rd Squadron, 10th ARVN Cavalry Regiment, pulls a companion vehicle out of the mud during operations near Sy Doi in June 1967. The leading APC mounts an M74 machine-gun turret, one of several types of cupola fitted to ARVN carriers to provide greater protection to the gunner. (US Army)

20. With boxes of small arms ammunition laid across the glacis plate behind an engineer stake, an M41A3 stands guard in the outskirts of Saigon during the 'mini-Tet' offensive of May 1968. Unusually this tank carries above the main armament an AN-VSS-1 searchlight of the type fitted to US Marine Pattons. (Tim Page)

21. A heavily laden M577 Command Vehicle and an M113 APC of Task Force 255 advance into Cambodia during the incursion of 1970. Unlike American ACAVs, most ARVN APCs had no sideshields but simply lashed tripod-mounted .30in Brownings beside the troop compartment. (US Army)

22. M113 APCs of 10th Armored Cavalry Regiment move across dry paddy-fields in the Parrot's Beak area during the incursion into Cambodia in May 1970. Characteristically the trim vane is extended to provide a holder for stowage which also acted as additional protection against RPG fire. (US Army)

21▲ 22▼

▲23

▲24 ▼25

23. An M41A3 advances along Route 9 during the ARVN invasion of Laos to cut the Ho Chi Minh trail in 1971. Across the turret roof is draped an air recognition panel and on the glacis plate boxes of ammunition and a C-ration carton, which was unusual on ARVN vehicles because the Vietnamese did not favour Western food. (*Armor* Magazine)

24. The first American armoured units to arrive in Vietnam landed on 9 December 1964 at Da Nang where they acted as a reaction force to protect the airfield after a concerted Viet Cong attack on Bien Hoa airbase near Saigon. The US Marine Corps units were 3rd Platoon, Alpha Company, 3rd Tank Battalion; 1st Platoon, Alpha Company, 3rd Anti-Tank Battalion; and 1st Platoon, Bravo Company, 1st Amphibian Tractor Battalion. They are seen here at a Vietnamese Navy PT boat base below Monkey Mountain where they remained for a week before returning to Okinawa. (Gary Solis)

25. On 8 March 1965 American ground forces were fully committed to the Vietnam War when Battalion Landing Team 3/9 went ashore at Da Nang to form a part of the 9th Marine Expeditionary Brigade. In support were the M48AS tanks of 2nd Platoon, Bravo Company, 3rd Tank Battalion, commanded by Lieutenant F. Claybaugh. Here, the beachmaster in a US Navy DUKW directs amtracs and landing craft through the heavy surf on to Red Beach 2. (USMC)

26. An ARVN M41A3 of 1st Squadron, 5th Armored Cavalry Regiment, advances through the streets of Da Nang during the Buddhist revolt in the northern provinces of the Republic of Vietnam in May 1966. (Tim Page)

27. Originally conceived as an armoured personnel carrier, the M113 became a true fighting vehicle in Vietnam in the guise of the ACAV – Armored Cavalry Assault Vehicle. (John Graber)

28. Pattons and ACAVs of 3rd Squadron, 11th Armored Cavalry Regiment, protect the perimeter of the air base at Bien Hoa in late 1968. (Tom White)

29. The crew of a Centurion Mk 5/1 (AUST) of C Squadron, 1st Armoured Regiment, Royal Australian Armoured Corps, relax on their tank as a fire support base is constructed in the jungle of Phuoc Tuy Province in 1968. (Tom White)

30. An M48A3 of 3rd Platoon, Alpha Company, 3rd Tank Battalion, equipped with a deep fording kit, wades ashore from a Landing Craft Utility (LCU) at Chu Lai, May 1965. On this occasion, two tanks were landed from LCM-8s; the M48A3 of

the platoon commander, Lieutenant K. Zitz, was launched into twelve feet of water, way above the fording depth of the tank, but reached the shoreline safely. The remaining tanks in this LCU were dropped in shallower water, but in so doing one of its propellers was torn off. (USMC)

31. A column of LVTP-5 amphibian tractors ('amtracs') of Bravo Company, 1st Amphibian Tractor Battalion, roll along a beach near Chu Lai after landing with infantry on a 'search and clear' mission during July 1965. In the early years of the war amtracs were often employed as armoured personnel carriers during operations on land. (USMC)

▲32 ▼33

32. The first major battle involving Marine armour was Operation 'Starlite' in August 1965. The tank units were HQS, Charlie Company, 3rd Tank Battalion, acting as the tank command element; 1st Platoon, Alpha Company, 3rd Tank Battalion, commanded by Lieutenant W. Forney; and 3rd Platoon of the same company under Lieutenant K. Thompson. After wading ashore, the tanks were soon involved in a fierce firefight and three of them (A-31, A-32 and A-35) were knocked out by 75mm recoilless rifle fire – the first occasion on which this weapon had been encountered firing anti-tank ammunition. In addition, two M67A2 flame tanks were destroyed by RPGs (Rocket Propelled Grenades). In this picture a Marine crouches beside the bodies of the Viet Cong anti-tank team that knocked out the M48A3 (A-32), commanded by Sergeant Dan McCreay, in the background. (Tim Page)
33. Amtracs were also used during 'Starlite' but they suffered heavily from recoilless rifle and RPG fire,

particularly those which were ambushed during a resupply run near the village of An Cuong 2. Nine LVTP-5A1s were destroyed during 'Starlite'. An M51 Heavy Recovery Vehicle stands by to recover a knocked out amtrac from which Marine dead are being removed. (Tim Page)

34. 'Grunts' of Foxtrot Company, 2/3 Marines, disembark from an LVTP-5A of Bravo Company, 1st Amphibian Tractor Battalion, after crossing a river near Nam Yen during a 'Search and Kill' mission, May 1965. Limited fire support could be provided by the .30in Browning in the M1 machine-gun cupola (USMC)

35. LVTP-5A1 amtracs of 3rd Platoon, Bravo Company, 1st Amphibian Tractor Battalion, carrying H/2/3 Marines along the Ca De Son river to Pho Nan Thuong for a village search, June 1965. The numerous rivers in Vietnam proved to be no obstacle to amtracs and they were extensively employed on inland waterways to interdict VC/NVA supply sampans. (USMC)

▲36

36. An M53 of 1st 155 Gun Battery (SP) fires on enemy positions near Phu Bai, February 1967. These 155mm self-propelled howitzers were rarely employed in a mobile role and usually remained in static emplacements at fire-support bases. (USMC)

37. Members of the 3rd Platoon, 1st 8in Howitzer Battery (SP), prepare the gun of an M55 for firing. The M55 was identical with the M53 except for the main armament and ammunition stowage. The size of the propellant charge and the

M106 HE shell in the foreground identify this vehicle as an M55. (USMC)

38. An M67A3 flame thrower attached to Alpha Company, 3rd Tank Battalion, burns away vegetation bordering Route 9 between Cam Lo and Khe Sanh. Flame tanks were part of the Headquarters and Service Company of Marine tank battalions, but they were often attached to tank companies for specific operations or extended periods. The flame-gun had an effective range of approximately 150 metres. (USMC)

▲39   ▼40

39. An M48A3 of 3rd Tank Battalion disembarks from an LCM-8 'Mike Boat' at the Dong Ha ramp across the Qua Viet river, June 1967. On the glacis plate is the Fleet Marine Force tactical insignia for 3rd Tanks, a yellow shield with 3 TKS in red. (USMC)

40. One interesting variant of the LVTP-5A1 in Vietnam was the 'amcrash'. This vehicle was modified to carry fire equipment and serve at the Chu Lai airbase of Marine Air Group 12. It was used to reach aircraft crash sites beyond the runway in an area of loose sand inaccessible to wheeled fire tenders. (USMC)

41. M109 155mm self-propelled howitzers of M Battery, 4th Battalion, 12th Marines, move into position south of Phu Bai prior to a fire mission against suspected Viet Cong positions. (USMC)

42. An LVTP-5A1 is led by a 'ground guide' through the Marble Mountain base of 3rd Amphibian Tractor Battalion in 1968. By this time many amtracs had a sandbag emplacement forward of the M1 turret for better observation and a wider field of fire, and mounted either a .30in Browning or M60 machine-gun. (USMC)

43. With its 106mm recoilless rifles elevated, an M50A1 Ontos guards the perimeter of a Marine encampment in the Chu Lai area, May 1966. Designed as a light, air-portable tank destroyer, the Ontos was generally ineffectual in Vietnam. Because no enemy tanks were encountered, Ontos was employed for convoy escort, point security and perimeter defence. (USMC)

44. A Marine advances cautiously under sniper fire with an M48A3 (Late Model) in support in the University area of Hue during the vicious street fighting of the Tet offensive, February 1968. This Patton served with the Headquarters and Service Company of 3rd Tank Battalion, and was one of only four tanks available in the first days of the battle for Hue. (USMC)

45. Lurking among bamboo along the track north of 'Leatherneck Square', an M48A3 (Late Model) of 3rd Tank Battalion waits in readiness for any sign of the Viet Cong during Operation 'Kentucky' in support of 2/4 Marines, February 1968. The wire frame forward of the M1 cupola and vision block ring prevents the commander from firing his .50in machine-gun through the searchlight when it is mounted above the 90mm main gun. (USMC)

46. This intriguing photograph shows Pattons of 3rd Tank Battalion and M113 APCs in USMC markings on patrol west of Quang Tri Combat Base in January 1969. The Marines were not issued with M113s in Vietnam and the appearance of a Special Forces member on the rear carrier (infantrymen without helmet covers – unheard of in the Marines) and the Army camouflage pattern of the bush hat in the foreground suggests that this is a US Army unit introduced into I Corps Tactical Zone (with the aim of confusing the enemy as to the whereabouts of Marine Units). (USMC)

47. During the fighting in Hue, the Ontos gave valuable fire support against enemy positions. The Ontos unit involved was Alpha Company, 1st Anti-Tank

▼46 ▲47

Battalion, 1st Marine Division. This Ontos mounts only four of its recoilless rifles – the remaining two were damaged by RPG fire near the Province Capital building. The red marking A1 within a stencilled circle on the right front fender indicates 1st Platoon, Alpha Company, 1st Anti-Tank Battalion. The yellow figures below give the federal stock number for a fender flap. (USMC)

48. An LVTH-6A1 opens fire in support of ground troops during Operation 'Oklahoma Hills', April 1969. The 1st Provisional Armored Amphibian Platoon with six 'How Six' vehicles was formed experimentally in 1965, but was destined to remain in Vietnam until 1972 and became the last Marine armoured unit to serve in the war. (USMC)

48▲

▲49　▼50

49. An M88 VTR carries out an engine change in the field at Fire Support Base Andy in Quan Loi Province, 1969. A complete powerpack change could be achieved in under two hours. Typical of M88s in Vietnam, this VTR mounts no fewer than three .50in machine-guns forward of the crew hatches. (John Graber)

50. A pair of M88 VTRs lift a mine-damaged M48A3 of 11th Armored Cavalry Regiment on to the rear bed of a tank transporter by means of the front mounted A-frame boom. (John Graber)

51. DRAFT DODGER, an ACAV of Delta Company, 11th Armored Cavalry Regiment, bedecked in GT 'go-faster' stripes, illustrates the use of styrofoam floatation pods mounted on the front hull plate to compensate for the extra weight of 'belly armour' added to the hull floor to give greater protection from landmines. (John Graber)

52. A column of APCs from Company B, 1st Battalion, 5th Infantry (Mechanized) of 25th Infantry Division advances across a rice paddy during Operation 'Kalamazoo' near Cu Chi, April 1966. These M113s are fitted with 'Okinawa gunshields' for their .50in Brownings. The first standardised gunshields were manufactured at a US Army depot in Okinawa and were an interim measure until the introduction of the FMC ACAV kit. (US Army)

▲53

▲54 ▼55

53. ACAVs and Pattons of 3rd Squadron, 11th Armored Cavalry Regiment, return fire into the treeline as snipers rake a section of M106A1 self-propelled mortars during Operation 'Hickory', October 1966. Mortar carriers can be identified by the side-opening, folding roof hatches. Both these M106A1s have the 'B Model' turret and sub-system and each is equipped with a single M60 behind a gunshield. The shield was not originally intended for 'mortar tracks' but was commonly fitted in the field. Unit markings have been obscured by mud to subdue the prominent white stars which formed a conspicuous aiming-point for RPG gunners. (US Army)

54. A Scorpion 90mm SPAT (Self-Propelled Anti-Tank gun) of Company D, 16th Armor, passes members of Company A, 2nd Battalion, 503rd Infantry, 173rd Airborne Brigade, during Operation 'New Life', November 1965. The SPAT was a light assault vehicle for airborne units, later superseded by the Sheridan. (US Army)

55. An M48A3 and an ACAV lead a truck convoy carrying men of Company A, 2nd Battalion, 327th Infantry, 101st Airborne Division, from Camp Eagle to Fire Support Base Bastogne, June 1969. Convoy escort through the uncommanded Vietnamese road network was a routine mission for armoured units. (US Army)

56. A battery of M107 175mm self-propelled guns prepares to open fire in support of Marines during an operation in 1967. With a range of 32 kilometres, the M107 provided artillery support over wide areas from fire bases located throughout the Republic of Vietnam. (USMC)

57. An M48A3 (Late Model) of 3rd Platoon, Company A, 1st Battalion, 69th Armor, pulls out of Landing Zone 'Pat' in the Central Highlands, April 1969. The squadron insignia and callsign number was painted high on the turret sides where it was obscured by dust, mud, ration boxes or the spare trackblocks carried for protection from RPGs. (US Army)

56▲   57▼

▲58 ▼59

58. Protected by an earthwork berm, an M551 Sheridan of 2nd Squadron, 11th Armored Cavalry Regiment, stands on the perimeter of Firebase Fiddler's Green. This Sheridan has a second M2HB Browning at the loader's hatch and, as with many Sheridans in Vietnam, its flotation screen and splash board have been removed. These items were easily damaged when operating in jungle. (Armor Magazine)

59. AFVs of 1st Brigade, 5th Infantry Division (Mechanized) are refuelled during Operation 'Utah Mesa' in the A Shau Valley, July 1969. Here, an M578 light recovery vehicle lifts fuel drums from an M548 tracked load carrier. The M548 was used as a resupply vehicle carrying general cargo, ammunition or fuel to armoured units operating in hostile terrain beyond the reach of wheeled trucks. (US Army)

60. An M48A3 (Late Model) Patton of 1st Squadron, 11th Armored Cavalry Regiment, undergoes maintenance in the field at Quan Loi in 1969. (John Graber)

61. Shrouded in the red dust characteristic of much of Vietnam, M551 Sheridans of 1st Squadron, 11th Armored Cavalry Regiment, are prepared for action at Quan Loi in 1969. (John Graber)

▲62 ▼63

62. Australian M113A1 APCs of 3rd Cavalry Regiment move through typical terrain during an operation in Phuoc Tuy Province in 1971. (Doug Lennox)

63. The M60 Main Battle Tank did not serve in Vietnam, but two variants, the AVLB and the CEV, were employed in their specialised roles. An M728 Combat Engineer Vehicle of the 919th Engineer Battalion stands among the trees in Quan Loi during 1969. (John Graber)

64. Sporting the name BIG JOHN on its trim vane, an M577A1 of 1st Brigade, 5th Infantry Division (Mechanized), moves through the A Shau Valley, a long-standing stronghold, during Operation 'Utah Mesa', July 1969. Based on the M113, the M577 had an enlarged hull for use by field commanders as a command and communications vehicle (US Army)

65. With its suspension system clogged with rice shoots and glutinous mud, an APC of Company A, 5th Battalion, 60th Infantry (Mechanized) of 9th Infantry Division, pulls a companion vehicle out of a paddy-field during Operation 'Coronado 5' south of Cai Lay, September 1967. This task was undertaken countless times during mobile operations, and tow cables were expended at a prodigious rate. (*Armor* Magazine)

64▲   65▼

66. The crew of an M551 Sheridan of 1st Squadron, 1st Cavalry, carry out engine maintenance in the field. Despite its size the Sheridan lacked internal stowage space for the crew's personal belongings so the exterior was often festooned with all manner of impedimenta. Frequently a cut-down 152mm ammunition box was fixed along the turret side above the grenade launchers and stacked with oil cans and ration cartons (*Armor* Magazine)

67. M113 APCs of 1st Battalion, 5th Infantry (Mechanized), 25th Infantry Division, churn through an abandoned rubber plantation. This carrier has the 'Okinawa' type hatch armour for the commander but lacks a gunshield for its .50in Browning (*Armor* Magazine)

68. At the completion of an operation in support of the 101st Airborne Division, an M48A3 (and mascot) of Company C, 2nd Battalion, 34th Armor, returns to Camp Evans near Hue. Note the sandbags laid on the front trackguards to absorb mine blast and the M2 Browning on an M3 tripod welded above the commander's cupola. (*Armor* Magazine)

69. Mines – the principal threat to AFVs in Vietnam. A column of smoke and dust rises from an M48A3 of 2nd Battalion, 34th Armor which has struck a mine during an operation in 1967. (US Army)

70. The majority of M48 tanks survived mine attack without damage to their interiors and usually suffered only the loss of roadwheels, torsion bars and trackblocks. The crew of this M48A3 have succeeded in reconnecting the track after losing the front roadwheel, only to hit another mine 200 metres down the road. (*Armor* Magazine)

68▲

69▲ 70▼

71

71. A line of M48A3 Pattons of Company C, 2nd Battalion, 34th Armor, await fire orders during an operation in conjunction with the 101st Airborne Division near Hue. Each of these Pattons has a stowage rack fabricated from engineers' stakes over the engine decks – a common modification on the tanks of this battalion. (*Armor* Magazine)

72. AFVs of 1st Battalion, 5th Infantry Division (Mechanized), negotiate difficult terrain in the Khe Sanh area with the aid of an Armored Vehicle Launched Bridge during Operation 'Utah Mesa' in June 1969. On the skyline is an M48A3 Patton covering the progress of these two M106 mortar carriers and an ACAV. (US Army)

72 **73**

73. Grinding through the mud of a swollen stream, an M113 APC of 4th Battalion (Mechanized), 23rd Infantry of 25th Infantry Division, returns to a Night Defensive Position near Memot during the incursion into Cambodia in 1970. When operating in such close terrain there was the ever present danger of enemy RPG teams. (*Armor* Magazine)

74. 'Firing now!' An M107 of A Battery, 2nd Battalion, 94th Artillery of 108th Artillery Group, fires in support of Marines operating in the A Shau Valley in August 1967. The 175mm self-propelled guns of the US Army's 2/94th Arty were introduced into I Corps Tactical Zone to give heavy artillery support over wider areas than was possible using Marine artillery. (USMC)

75. The crew of an M106 mortar carrier of 2nd Battalion (Mechanized), 47th Infantry of 9th Infantry Division, fires a 4.2in (107mm) round in support of infantry during a 'reconnaissance in force' in September 1968. The mortar base plate on the side of the M106 identifies the 'four-deuce' from the M125 81mm self-propelled mortar which also served in mechanized infantry battalions. (US Army)

76. Weaving their way through the trees of an abandoned rubber plantation, ACAVs and Sheridans of Troop C, 1st Squadron, 11th Armored Cavalry Regiment, conduct a 'search and destroy' mission near Loc Ninh in January 1970. The regulated distance between rubber trees allowed relatively free movement for AFVs through these plantations. Note the rectangular rack holding 'mini-gun' boxes and water jerrycans on the rear hulltop, carried by many Sheridans to augment the limited stowage space. (US Army)

▲75   ▼76

77. HARDCORE – an ACAV of Company H, 2nd Squadron, 11th Armored Cavalry Regiment, moves through a suspected VC village during a 'search and destroy' mission in conjunction with the 196th Light Infantry during Operation 'Hood River' in August 1967. (US Army)
78. 'Circle the Wagons' – M48A3 Pattons of Company M, 3rd Squadron, 11th Armored Cavalry Regiment, set up a Night Defensive Position after reaching their objective during Operation 'Hickory', east of Bien Hoa in October 1966. Each of the three armoured cavalry squadrons of 11ACR had an attached company of 27 M48 tanks for greater firepower and 'jungle-busting' capability. (US Army)

77▲ 78▼

▲79 ▼80

79. An M48A3 Patton of 1st Battalion, 69th Armor, transports a long-range reconnaissance patrol of 4th Infantry Division towards the Cambodian border in May 1967. Note the wire guard forward of the commander's cupola to prevent the searchlight being riddled by the .50in machine-gun. (US Army)

80. Although intended for air defence, the three battalions of M42 40mm self-propelled anti-aircraft guns sent to Vietnam were deployed in a number of roles including convoy escort, perimeter defence and point security. An M42A1 'Duster' of 5th Battalion, 2nd Artillery, fires on a target in III Corps Tactical Zone. (US Army)

81. Working in close co-operation, an M48A3 Patton of 2nd Battalion, 34th Armor, and troops from 2nd Battalion, 14th Infantry, search for sniper positions during an operation north of Cu Chi in 1969. As with most tanks in Vietnam this Patton carries an RPG screen of cyclone fencing across the engine covers. In defensive positions this device was erected forward of the tank to protect it from rocket attack. (*Armor* Magazine)

▲82 ▼83

82. Self-propelled artillery weapons were rarely employed on mobile operations in Vietnam because of their vulnerability to mines and RPGs. They were usually confined to static positions in fire support bases as with this M107 from 8th Battalion, 4th Artillery, at Fire Support Base 'Sheraton Rockpile' in 1969. (US Army)

83. Troopers of 11th Armored Cavalry Regiment halt their M48A3 Pattons in Quan Loi for a five-day stand-down over Christmas at the end of a mission in 1969. To overcome the problems of operating the commander's heavy machine-gun inside his cramped cupola most tanks had the Browning mounted on top. (US Army)

84. Of all the tracked vehicles used in Vietnam, none had a greater impact on the landscape than the 'Rome Plows' of engineer land-clearing companies. Employed to clear vast tracts of jungle and undergrowth hiding enemy base camps and infiltration routes, the Rome Plow was a standard Caterpillar medium crawler tractor fitted with a special tree-felling blade. A Rome Plow from 59th Engineer Company clears a hillside of vegetation in the Chu Lai area in January 1971. (US Army)

85. A truck convoy carrying troops from the 101st Airborne Division moves out from Camp Eagle for Fire Base Bastogne under the protection of ACAVs and an M4A3 (Late Model). Armoured units spent almost a third of their time escorting truck convoys over the insecure road network in Vietnam. (US Army)

86. In the typically hostile terrain encountered in Vietnam, an M48A3 Patton forces its way through dense undergrowth to clear a path for M113 APCs. The 'jungle-busting' capability of the M48 was a valuable contribution to the mobility of armoured units in thick jungle and allowed them to penetrate inaccessible areas in order to uncover enemy bases and sanctuaries. (US Army)

84▲

85▲   86▼

89▲

87. Sitting on a 'marmite' insulated food container, the track commander of an M113 from Company A, 2nd Battalion, 22nd Infantry (Mechanized), consults his map as the crew prepare to move out during Operation 'Yellowstone' in January 1968. The M113 is fitted with 'stand-off' armour along the sides of the hull as added protection against RPGs. (US Army)

88. Loaded down with ammunition boxes, ration cartons and the obligatory RPG screen, an M551 Sheridan of E Company, 1st Cavalry, fords a river in Quang Ngai Province in June 1971. The Sheridan began to replace the M48 in divisional armoured cavalry squadrons from early 1969. (US Army)

89. Infantrymen assist the crew members of an M88 VTR of 1st Squadron, 1st Cavalry, as they attach a winch cable to a bogged-down M48A3 Patton during an operation near Tam Ky in December 1967. The M88 was the principal recovery vehicle of maintenance personnel in armoured units and it performed yeoman service in Vietnam. (US Army)

▲90 ▼91

90. Moving through terrain devastated by bombs and artillery fire, a heavily laden M551 Sheridan leads an armoured column during an operation in the Northern Provinces. Sheridan crew members frequently rode on the outside of the vehicle because of the heat, for fear of mines and for better observation. (*Armor Magazine*)

91. M113 APCs from the 1st Brigade, 5th Infantry Division (Mechanized), pass an M60 Armored Vehicle Launched Bridge during Operation 'Utah Mesa' in the A Shau Valley, a long-standing VC/NVA stronghold, in July 1969. (US Army)

92. On account of the losses incurred from mine damage and in ambushes, many transportation units added armour protection to their trucks. This expedient proved effective against ambushes, but the toll from mines remained high. 'Hardened trucks' of 57th Transportation Battalion carry Marines providing security for a convoy between Dong Ha to Ca Lu, just south of the DMZ, in April 1968. (USMC)

▲93   ▼94

93. Firing for effect, an M48A3 of Company A, 2nd Battalion, 34th Armor, engages enemy positions near Tay Ninh City. Spare trackblocks were affixed around the turret as a counter to RPGs. This tank carries rolls of cyclone fencing and an observer's seat on the rear decks. (*Armor* Magazine)

94. With the name 'Eve of Destruction' painted on the gunshield of the .50in Browning and flying a pennant emblazoned with a Martini glass and the legend 'Happy Hour', an ACAV of 3rd Squadron, 5th Cavalry, takes up a defensive ambush position on the road between Mai Loc and Fire Support Base 'Holcomb' in August 1970. (US Army)

95. A tanker convoy from the 8th Transportation Group *en route* to An Khe passes ACAVs from 2nd Squadron, 1st Cavalry, along Route 19 in May 1970. The ACAVs are deployed in 'herringbone formation' to present maximum firepower to the flanks in case of ambush. (US Army)

96. In order to increase driver protection in APCs from mine explosions, some units extended the primary controls so that the driver rode on top of the vehicle where he was less vulnerable to mine blast. Known as 'Long Controls', this expedient impeded the commander's field of fire and also exposed the driver to small arms fire. (US Army)

U S ARMY
13D-061

▲97 ▼98

97. The amphibious capability of the M113 was a major asset in Vietnam where the numerous waterways were a formidable obstacle to motorized and armoured units. The APC was capable of negotiating rivers without preparation as evidenced by these waterborne carriers in the early years of the conflict. (FMC)

98. The crew members of an M551 Sheridan from Troop E, 17th Cavalry, scan the treeline as they advance in support of troops of the 173rd Airborne Brigade in Binh Dinh Province. The powerful 152mm main armament of the Sheridan firing high explosive and cannister rounds was devastating against field fortification and enemy personnel. (*Armor* Magazine)

99. 'Turning on the rock 'n roll' – ACAVs and infantry advance against entrenched enemy positions. The standard armament of the ACAV was an M2HB .50in Browning and two side-mounted M60 machine-guns behind gunshields and armour protection for the vehicle commander. The ACAV kit, produced by FMC, was fitted to many M113s in Vietnam. (FMC)

99▼

100. An ACAV and an M48A3 from Troop C, 1st Squadron, 4th Cavalry of 1st Infantry Division, turn over security of a resupply convoy to Troop M, 3rd Squadron, 11th Armored Cavalry Regiment, north of Fire Support Base 'Hartman' on Highway 13 in September 1969. (US Army)

101. Troops of the 'Screaming Eagles' 101st Airborne Division advance across a paddy-field with ACAVs in support. In Vietnam, the M113 APC was used in greater numbers than any other armoured vehicle, while in its ACAV configuration it was employed as a true fighting vehicle in a light tank role. (FMC)

104 ▲

102. An M551 Sheridan of 1st Squadron, 11th Armored Cavalry Regiment, stands guard on the perimeter of a camp in III Corps Tactical Zone in 1969. Along the side of the vehicle is the name 'BODY COUNT' painted in red lettering outlined in white. Most Sheridans in Vietnam were fitted with a large stowage rack around the rear of the turret. (Geoff Cornish)
103. Many AFVs in Vietnam were fitted with additional machine-guns. BODY COUNT mounts two .50in Brownings at the commander's position in place of the usual one, and two

7.62mm M73 machine-guns at the loader's hatch. Across the gunshield are the further names 'BLOOD AND GUTS' and 'THE STALKING RHINO'. (Geoff Cornish)
104. On many occasions it was not possible to retrieve bogged APCs with conventional recovery vehicles because of the marshy terrain. One spectacular method of recovery which proved effective in such circumstances was to use a CH-47 Chinook helicopter to lift the stranded APC out of the mire. (*Armor* Magazine)

▲105

105. Tanks and APCs were not always available to act as convoy escorts so transportation units armed and armoured some of their vehicles for self-protection such as this M54 5-ton truck mounting M55 quad .50in machine-guns as it prepares to move out with a convoy to Ban Me Thuot in September 1970. (US Army)

106. The M706 V-100 Commando armoured car was employed by both the ARVN and the US Army in Vietnam for convoy escort and police duties. Built by Cadillac-Gage, the V-100 was known as 'the Duck' from its pointed front and rear. (Geoff Cornish)

▲106

107. On their arrival in Vietnam, Australian M113A1 APCs were armed with a .50in Browning machine-gun on a simple pintle mount to which was added a gunshield for the vehicle commander. Subsequently many APCs were fitted with machine-gun turrets, such as the Cadillac-Gage M74C version illustrated here, which provided greater protection. (Doug Lennox)

108. Early in 1968, a squadron of Centurion tanks of 1st Armoured Regiment, Royal Australian Armoured Corps, was dispatched to Vietnam to reinforce 1st Australian Task Force in Phuoc Tuy Province. Here, the Centurions of 2 Troop, C Squadron, are loaded aboard the SS *Japerit* at Sydney, January 1968. (1st Armoured Regiment, RAAC)

109. The Centurions of C Squadron conduct a fire mission against enemy positions during an operation around the Long Hai Hills in the south of Phuoc Tuy Province, March 1968. The accurate fire support by tanks against enemy bunker complexes and fortified positions contributed significantly to the success of numerous infantry operations. (Peter de Jong)

107▲

108▲ 109▼

▲110

▲111 ▼112

110. Tanks in Vietnam faced many hazards, not least of which was the primitive road system. This Centurion Mark 5/1 (AUST) came to grief when the roadside collapsed under its 50-ton weight. The Centurions that fought in Vietnam were modified from Mk 5 standard by the addition of a 100-gallon auxiliary fuel tank at the rear, additional armour on the glacis plate, night-fighting equipment and a .50in ranging gun in the mantlet. The tank's designation was Centurion Mk 5/1 (Australian). (Peter de Jong)

111. The dense jungles of Vietnam were a formidable obstacle to AFVs and only tanks were capable of forcing a path through such terrain. In this photograph one can see two Centurions separated by no more than a tank's width – a graphic indication of the problems of maintaining formation and observing enemy positions in such dense jungle growth. (Peter de Jong)

112. During Operation 'Cookdown Orchid' in April 1968, one Centurion was modified to clear an area of anti-personnel mines formerly laid by Australian engineers and which the Viet Cong now regarded as a convenient arsenal of mines for use against their original owner! This rare view shows the heavy I-beams and trailing chains of this naval configuration which did not prove very successful in practice. (Directorate of Armour)

113. A Centurion Mk 5/1 (AUST) of 1 Troop, B Squadron, is refuelled from rubber bladders during an operation near the Long Hai Hills in 1969. The carrier to the left is an M113A1 Fitter's Vehicle with a hydraulic lifting crane to carry out repairs and assembly changes in the field in support of the tank and APC squadrons. (Australian War Memorial)

114. The Australian tank squadron in Vietnam was supplemented by a Special Equipment Troop of Centurion Bridgelayers and Tankdozers. Besides its primary role of spanning gullies and watercourses, the bridgelayer was used as an infantry transport in relatively safe areas. (Australian War Memorial)

▲115 ▼116

115. The tanks and APCs of 1st Australian Task Force ranged all over Phuoc Tuy Province in search of the elusive enemy, rooting out his base camps and destroying bunker positions. In this photograph, Centurions and APCs ravage crops and cereals grown by the Viet Cong in the Binh Chuon jungle zone in eastern Phuoc Tuy Province. The plants were crushed by the AFV tracks, soaked in diesel fuel and set alight. (Peter de Jong)

116. In addition to the vehicles of the Special Equipment Troop, the Centurion squadron was supported by a Light Aid Detachment equipped with the Centurion ARV Mk 2 and the M113A1 Fitter's Vehicle. In this photograph, a Centurion Bridgelayer deploys its bridge over an obstacle while a Centurion ARV pauses in the foreground. (Doug Lennox)

117. On the shores of the South China Sea, an M113A1 APC of B Squadron, 3rd Cavalry Regiment, and a pair of M42A1 Duster 40mm self-propelled guns give protection to a working party of Royal Australian Engineers. In the foreground is an engineer Caterpillar D8 bulldozer fitted with an armoured cab to protect the operator from mines and small arms fire. (Doug Lennox)

118. The Centurions of 2 Troop, A Squadron, and the M113A1 of 3 Troop, B Squadron, 3rd Cavalry Regiment, provide support to C Company, 8th Royal Australian Regiment, during Operation 'Hammersley' against the Viet Cong D445 Battalion in the Minh Dam Secret Zone of the Long Hai Hills, February 1970. The tanks went in ahead of the APCs to detonate numerous mines and boobytraps; when this was done the infantry dismounted. Unusually for Australian troops, these men are wearing steel helmets and flak jackets, an indication of the real danger from mines. (Directorate of Armour)

117▲ 118▼

119. Among the standard modifications made to Centurions in Vietnam were the removal of the bazooka plates and shortening of the trackguards to prevent vegetation accumulating around the suspension and the fitting of engineer stakes to protect the latches of the stowage bins. Water jerrycans were carried across the transmission covers for ready replenishment in the field. On top of the auxiliary fuel tank of this Centurion are a fuel transfer pump and a refuelling hose. (Australian War Memorial)

120. M113A1s of 3 Troop, A Squadron, 3rd Cavalry Regiment, negotiate muddy terrain during an operation in Phuoc Tuy Province in 1971. These APCs are fitted with Cadillac-Gage T-50 turrets; the example in the foreground has been modified by moving the .50in M2HB Browning to the right-hand aperture and mounting the .30in on the roof for greater flexibility. Note the insignia of 1st Australian Task Force on the front plate. (Doug Lennox)

▲119 ▼120

121. In late 1970, an M48A3 equipped with an ENSURE 202 mine-roller was lent by the Americans to the Royal Australian Engineers; the vehicle, 92 Tango, is seen here sweeping a road in Phuoc Tuy Province. This equipment proved moderately successful until, ironically, it reversed over a mine and was disabled. (Doug Lennox)

122. An M113A1 Fitter's Vehicle renders assistance to a Centurion Mk 5 Tankdozer. This versatile variant of the standard APC featured a hydraulic crane for replacing components in the field. A replacement Centurion Meteor engine or an M113 powerpack could be carried in the rear compartment, together with other replacement parts. (Doug Lennox)

121▲ 122▼

▲123

123. An AN/PRC 524 radio set is lifted aboard a Centurion in 'Sydney Opera House', the tank workshop at the Australian base camp in Nui Dat. On the glacis plate are spare roadwheels to offset the risk of mine damage. The gun barrel bears the legend UPTIGHT at the breech and OUT OF SIGHT at the muzzle. (Australian War Memorial)

124. On 8 September 1971 a farewell parade was held at Nui Dat on the departure of the Australian tank squadron from Vietnam. At 1100 hours the last Centurion to leave 'the Dat' (169017 'CENTAUR') dipped its gun in salute to the Deputy Commander of 1st Australian Task Force, Colonel D. D. Weir, who declared, 'This Task Force will never forget the squadrons of 1st Armoured Regiment, but similarly nor will 33rd NVA Regiment, 274 VC Regiment, D445 VC Battalion and sundry others.' (Australian War Memorial)

▼124